The Way We Were

RABBIT HOUSE PRESS
Versailles, KY 40383

Copyright © 1997 by Jonelle Fisher

Published in 2025 by Rabbit House Press.

All rights reserved. No part of this book may be reproduced in any form or by any electronic or mechanical means, including information storage and retrieval systems, without permission in writing from the author, except by a reviewer who may quote brief passages in review with attribution.

Published in the United States of America by Rabbit House Press, September 2025.

ISBN: 979-8-9929838-3-8

Editor: Erin Chandler
Interior/cover design & formatting; copy editor: Brooke Lee

Other books by Jonelle Jones Fisher:

Ahead of the Hounds (1988, 2024)

A Soul Remembering (1999)

Morning's at Seven (2001, 2025)

For All Times (2002)

Nantura (2004)

MacKenzie Miller, The Gentleman Trainer from Morgan Street (2006)

Dedicated to the memory of my sister, Ann Bowling, because it could not have been a book without her remarkable memory and her willingness to put it all down on two tapes for me to use. She not only had the memories, but she had a wonderful way of telling a story. We had an unusual childhood together, and it created a bond between us that was everlasting.

I'm also greatly indebted to the memory of my mother, Mary Jones, and my cousin, Jack Greene, for their invaluable input into these remembrances.

This book was first written for family in the mid-1990s but was not published until the autumn of 2025. I have tried in every instance to be honest in the writing of it—the stories are written exactly as Ann, Jack or I remembered them. If you recall things differently and think I am mistaken about something, you must never tell me. I have a divine right not to know.

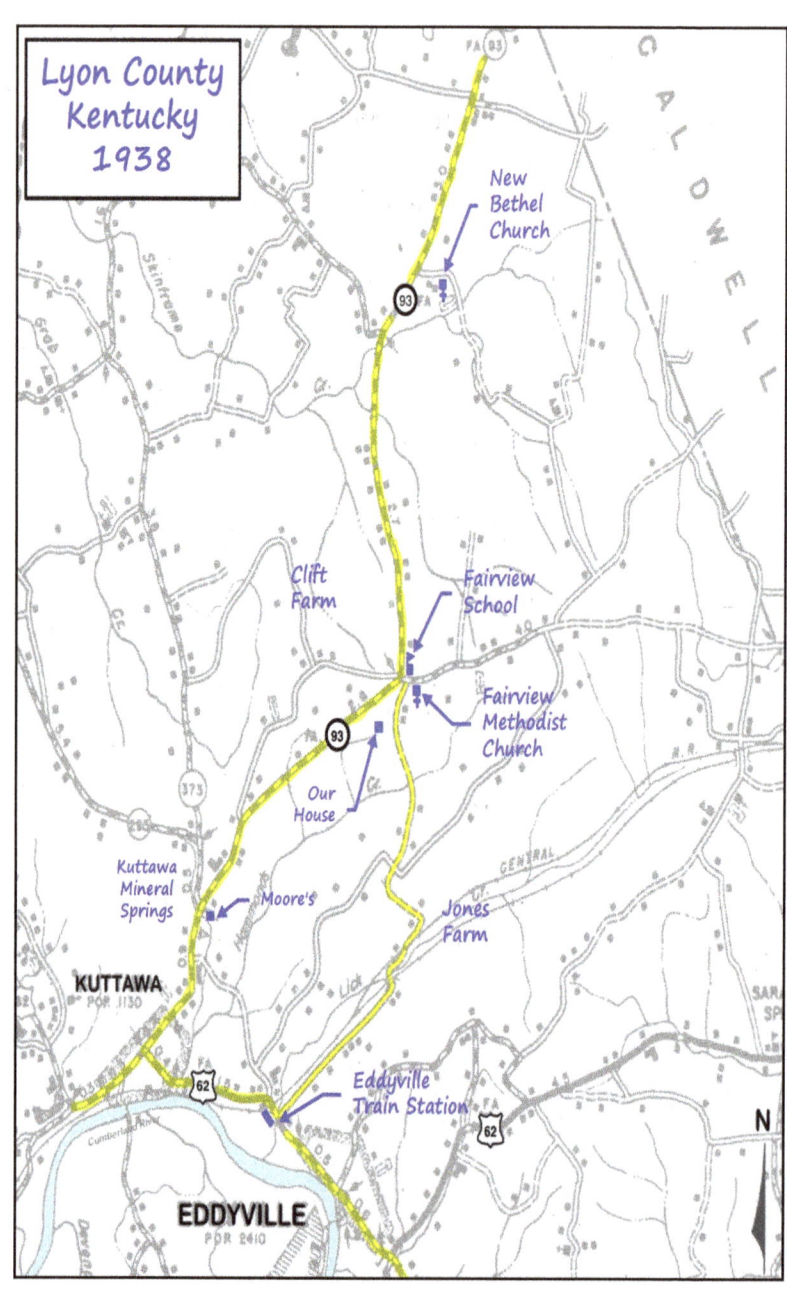

The Way We Were

Jonelle Jones Fisher

*Backward, turn backward,
Oh Time, in your flight,
Make me a child again
Just for tonight!*

Elizabeth A. Allen
Rock Me to Sleep

Ann

Jack

Jo

CONTENTS

CHAPTER I: **Balances** | 1

CHAPTER II: **Places of the Heart** | 5

CHAPTER III: **The Four of Us** | 15

CHAPTER IV: **The Jones Clan** | 25

CHAPTER V: **The Clift Family** | 41

CHAPTER VI: **Dear Old Golden Rule Days** | 53

CHAPTER VII: **Special Times** | 65

CHAPTER VIII: **The Way We Were** | 73

CHAPTER IX: **"Farewell to the Farm"** | 83

APPENDIX:

   My Dad's Vocabulary | 89
   A Place | 91
   About the Author | 95

CHAPTER I

BALANCES

"Life is full of balances" is a truism that my brother-in-law, Jim Bowling, quoted to me frequently. Through the years I have found that opinion is absolutely correct. And there could be no truer statement that I could make about my family's life in rural Lyon County during the years between 1933 when I was born—and 1945, at which time we pulled up stakes and moved to Louisville for Daddy to take a job with the Internal Revenue Service. Our life on the farm three miles from the town of Kuttawa was one of hardships and one of joy. On the hardship side, it was just following the depression, and there was never money to spare. Everybody in the family had to work to make a go of it, even the children. We had very few toys, Mama made most of our clothes, and our food came from the land and from animals there on the farm. We had more than our share of sickness—Ann had diphtheria, we both had Scarlet Fever, and I very nearly died from Colitis when I was two years old. We were bitten by our old dog Max, who was rabid at the time, and we both had to take the rabies shots that were so dangerous in that day. The following year, Ann was pecked by a rabid chicken and had to repeat the terrifying shots. We had very few creature comforts as there was no running water, telephone service, or electricity on the farm—or on anybody's farm in that area. The land in Lyon County was not ideally suited for farming, and farming was what both sides of our family did for a living. It was very hard work, and Daddy never had any mechanized machinery to make it easier. I often heard him say, "It was a good year—I managed to break even," and I was never sure that he was kidding.

However, on the "balance" side, we were an unusual family in that we all cared deeply about one another—and I don't mean just the immediate family or the four of us—we cared for our grandparents, aunts and uncles, and our cousins, and they cared back. We would enjoy being with family on either side more than anyone else whether at Mom Clift's or at Grandmother's. Had the Jones Clan had a lot of money and power, we probably could have been compared with the Kennedys because of the deep and abiding love we felt for one another, along with an overwhelming hot competitive streak in each of us when we were pitted against other family members in our "games." I was the youngest cousin on both sides, and it was a tough row to hoe, just trying to carve out a spot for myself during the competitive bouts of Rook, soft ball, Easter egg hunting, Crokinole, or what-have-you, one of which would be going on every single time we ever went to Grandmother Jones'. The competition was relentless—with adults usually included—and there was no quarter given just because we were children. And none asked, I might add. The pace was more relaxing at Mom

Clift's where we would usually watch her cook and she would show us how to do the things she was doing. She taught us how to put apples and peaches on the roof of her lumber room to dry to make her pies; how to take a silver spoon to lift the guinea eggs out of the nest so the hen would not smell a human hand in her nest and would lay there again; and she taught us how to make hooked rag rugs. She would also let us play on her piano or organ, no matter how much noise we made. She never tired of our "music."

Another "balance" was that we ate well. Mama had a huge garden just at the back of the house and we ate vegetables and fruit every day, and it seemed like there was not a meal put on the table without fried chicken. She canned all summer long. And it was enough to carry us through the long, hard winters. Hogs were killed every November, so pork was plentiful all year round—and when the time was right, Daddy hunted rabbits and squirrels, which we enjoyed. Grandfather fished a lot, and we always shared some of his catch—except we didn't like eating it as much as we could have because Mama was frantic that we would get a bone caught in our throats. We ate fish with fear and trepidation, but we still ate it.

We were always warm in the wintertime. We had a stove in the main room of our house where the fire blazed all day and steeped at night. Daddy would get up early enough in the morning to have the room toasty warm for us to dress to go to school. Years later when we lived in Louisville, he and Mama bought a house with a lovely fireplace in it. When my husband asked him why he never once built a fire in it, Daddy replied that he had done that every morning for forty-nine years, and he would never do it again unless he had to. Then he grinned and walked over to the thermostat on the wall and flipped it up to seventy-two degrees. Mom Clift had a stove like ours at her house, and we all would sit around it and talk for hours, children and adults alike. Grandmother's house had coal grates, and they put out a powerful heat that was wonderful to back up to when you came in out of the cold.

One other bonus on the good side of the "balance" was that all our neighbors were in the same boat. The time was hard throughout the area and no family escaped it. This was probably one of the reasons that neighbors were so good and caring with one another, all sharing good times and bad. There was a true spirit of community at that time in Lyon County. All in all, it was a wonderful life. I feel so privileged to have lived when and where I did. It very nearly broke my heart to leave it when I was eleven years old. I'm excited to be writing down what is remembered about those kinder and less complicated times.

CHAPTER II

PLACES OF THE HEART

In the summer of 1956, Congress appropriated money for the Army Corps of Engineers to build a dam on the Cumberland River that would flood part of Lyon County with a huge body of water that would become Barkley Lake. One problem with this was that the only two towns in the county, Eddyville and Kuttawa, would be mostly put under water, and the people and businesses of the towns would have to relocate. After long discussions on the matter the citizens of Eddyville decided to move out to the Fairview area and relocate their town. All that would be left of the old place would be the dominating Kentucky State Penitentiary on its hill, and a few houses that were situated near the prison and back behind it on a high ridge. The people of Kuttawa, after hemming and hawing for a while, finally decided not to join with Eddyville, but to relocate at Kuttawa Lake which was adjacent to the "Old" Kuttawa. So, the people who were left high and dry by the proposed Barkley Lake could use the same water and sewage lines and would be connected to the relocated town. The people of the two towns and the surrounding communities would now be able to make their living from the lake and tourism and would no longer be considered a farming locality.

The dam was dedicated in 1966 and the result was that most of my old landmarks of the towns I loved so much as a child were swallowed up, and the culture in the county was completely changed. The "balances" equation holds true in this situation I'm sure, but for me living up in Louisville at the time—the flooding of my beloved towns was a disaster. It wiped out some of the bedrock of my memories and when I go back now, I can't figure out just where I am in relation to the towns that I knew so well.

During the years from 1933 until 1945 when we were going "to town" on every Saturday possible, the place we went to was Kuttawa. It was a little town on the Cumberland River that had been founded by Charles Anderson, and it was most unusual. Mr. Anderson, a previous governor of Ohio, came to Kentucky at the end of the Civil War and purchased a large body of land, part of which would become the location of Kuttawa. He loved being near the river with a railroad close by, and he knew that some of this land contained valuable minerals. He moved to this area and made it his home until he died in 1893. He is buried in the old Kuttawa Cemetery with his wife, under a monument that is a concrete life-size replica of their bed with a coverlet of ivy. The bed is still standing there on the beautiful hillside looking out towards what has become Barkley Lake, although the old bed is in poor repair.

According to an article in the Courier Journal magazine of October 21st, 1956, it was the love for woods and fields that caused Governor Anderson to purchase the largest estate on the Cumberland River. On October 13th, 1895, the Courier stated: "He donated to the town ample grounds for public buildings, public squares and parks, and had it laid out with singular taste and judgment. If the citizens of Kuttawa will but carry out the plan of their benefactor, Kuttawa may become one of the most beautiful cities on the continent."

The Kuttawa that I remember from my childhood was just the place to be, come every Saturday afternoon. All the farmers and their neighbors would get in their cars and head to town to buy supplies and socialize on Saturday. As we would drive into town, the state highway became Oak Avenue, which was as wide as our four laned highway, with a median taken out of the middle that was planted with trees. We went in on a higher level than we left on, due to the high ridge rising up from the river—the river being just out of sight. Oak Avenue was thought of as being the most distinctive feature about the town. The median ended at about the place where the businesses began, but the wide street continued through the town. The businesses faced this broad avenue, and cars could be parked on a slant headed towards the buildings on both sides. It was always hard to find a place on Saturdays, but once you parked, you could stay all afternoon. People would stand all along the sidewalk and talk, as well as beside the cars, and even out in the street. At times they had drawings of silver dollars that would be held just off the main street at a certain time on Saturday afternoon. These were sponsored by the merchants, and you had to be present to win if they called your name. It seemed like hundreds of people would show up for these every week. The one time I wasn't there, my name was called for thirty-three silver dollars, and I still remember the feeling of disappointment that was mine because of missing the great thrill of getting to walk up in front of everybody and collect at a drawing. Not to mention the value of thirty-three silver dollars in those days.

The stores that I remember most were on the same side of town as Maddox's Grocery. That store was my favorite because every time I was in town, I would go in there and buy a huge slice of bologna with crackers, a pickle out of a barrel, and a soft drink—all for a dime. Life just didn't get any better than that. Then there was a shoe repair shop next to the Espie's cash store that sold shoes. Jack Greene (my cousin who will appear in this book with regularity as he was just one year older than I, and my boon companion) helped me to reconstruct the names of the businesses and this is what he came up with. Espie's was the place where his brother, Hugh Glenn (another buddy of mine although several years older) worked during his high school years. The top-of-the-line store in those days was Crosby Squares. Beyond Espie's was a store for taking in the cream that the farmers brought to town in the big old cans that were hard for anybody to lift. Then came Ed Jones who sold lumber, furniture, groceries, and so on. The barber, Harbine Glasgow, who cut my hair for a while, was next to the bank. Then came the drugstore with its Coca-Cola tables and chairs and the counter where I bought a strawberry ice cream cone every Saturday afternoon just before going home. Miss Julia Martin's was down the street, and this place was very important to my sister Ann, as it was a wonderful hang-out for teenagers. They had only popcorn, chips, cokes, and a jukebox, but they had booths where the young people could mingle and get to know one another. It was always crowded with the high schoolers and those even a little younger. I was sent in to get Ann every Saturday when it was time to go home, because we knew just where to look to find her. Tritt Jones' garage finished out this side of town.

On the other side of the street there was Wiseman's, then the Hotel with another barber in it. Ann and I must have been forbidden to go to the hotel, as I can't remember ever darkening the doors. The Post Office was over here, and Mama's cousin Randolph White was the Postmaster for years. The Hugh Wake and Company followed, with the slogan "Old Reliable" coming to Jack's mind. He seemed to think Wake's was considerably more expensive than Espie's and they sold shoes, suits, spools of thread, and such as that. Next was Standard Motors and it was up beside this place of business that the all-important drawings were held. There were some other stores, but we never went in them, and so they are forgotten.

One main reason I loved going to Kuttawa on a Saturday afternoon was that those hours were my special time with my Aunt Clara. She did all the shopping for Grandmother, and it was my delight to go from store to store with her and help her carry packages. When we moved to Louisville, she wrote me that her Saturdays in Kuttawa were just not the same without me and I cried myself to sleep that night.

As we would head home from Kuttawa, out from the town, past the Cemetery and on down a hill, we would come to J. I. Moore's, where Daddy often stopped for gas. We loved stopping because Moore's had delicious barbecue—pork and mutton—which they cooked in a deep pit at the back of the store. We could smell the pit way before we stopped, and we usually persuaded Daddy that we "needed" to have a sandwich.

The next familiar spot on the road was just on down, perhaps a half mile on the left-hand side of the road, and they had delicious barbecue also. It was just the pavilion at the Kuttawa

Mineral Springs, and it had been the center of much activity in its heyday. The first time my father took my mother out on a date, they drove down to the springs and back. It was quite the thing to do. Before I was born, or at least when I was too little to remember it, the springs had been used as a location for camp meetings, where people would come from miles around to hear traveling preachers hold a revival for two weeks, and there would be a lot of preaching, singing and socializing going on. Grandfather Jones bought a cabin there, just up the hill from the springs, which was a pretty nice place. He and Grandmother would move to the springs when the meetings were being held every summer, no matter what, even if there was hay left on the ground. The cabin had a place for croquet and a dirt tennis court that was never used. Several other families would move down to the springs at this time and there would be huge meals fixed and spread out under the trees. Ann remembers going there once and eating out on Grandfather's screened-in porch at a long table that had benches. That day Grandmother served pork and beans out of the can, something Ann had never tasted, and she thought they were marvelous and would eat nothing else. Ann also remembers a day at the springs when the family was on a blanket up high on a hill when she was very young, maybe four or five. She could look down on the mob of people, and as soon as she had the chance, she snuck away to mix with the crowd. "I was so happy. I don't know how long I was there, but I was just wandering around looking at bodies. Mama and Daddy missed me, and they were frantic. They thought I was kidnapped and came running down the hill, screaming until they found me."

Jack remembers a time when they would also be serving large amounts of ice cream at the pavilion on Sundays. He told me, "There would be three or four guys dipping, and as fast as they could dip it, it would be gone. They wouldn't even ask which flavor you wanted—there would be just strawberry, vanilla and chocolate. These guys would be dipping there and would say, 'Who wants it?' and it would be taken. One dip was a nickel and two were a dime."

At the point where the spring water surfaced, they built a concrete fixture that channeled the water out of large holes in several places. The water was absolutely pure, and ice cold to drink at any time. It also felt fantastic when you would stick your face under one of the spouts and let the bracing water rinse off your sweaty face when you were too hot from running, as we so often were.

By the time I can remember it, the springs had gone out of fashion, but you could still get a delicious barbecue sandwich by just going through the old squeaking door into the pavilion. I guess the deep smokey smell is the thing I remember the most.

Eddyville, the county seat of Lyon, was the only other town in the county, and it was just a little bigger than Kuttawa. Eddyville was an old town, having been laid out in 1799 by David Walker. It served as the county seat for each of the three counties that it found itself in—Livingston, Caldwell, and finally in Lyon in 1854.

In the forties, the prison was as overpowering in the landscape as it is today. It looked like a medieval castle, as it was made out of massive blocks of grey Kentucky limestone, and every window was covered with bars. Our aunt and uncle, Esh and Chester Cummins, lived just across the street sideways from this monstrosity. We were told never to look at the prisoners who would be watching us from the windows as we went into the house. I did what I was told and never even glanced up, but Ann says that she used to wait until Mama and Daddy were not looking, then she would look over her shoulder and wave at the prisoners. One of my first memories was of an election day when Mama and Daddy had to work at the polls, and they were taking us to Eshie's to stay. As we drew in front of the prison in our car, Daddy yelled at us "GET DOWN!!" and we dived to the floor in the back seat. But not before we had seen a man with a gun hiding behind a parked car, trying to make a getaway. Guards had their guns on him, as he was waiting for our car to come along to try to make a break for it. Thank God he didn't make it. Daddy made a beeline for Eshie's house.

We were taken to Eddyville regularly because Esh and Chester lived there. He was a guard at the prison on and off for many years. They had no children and doted on us as if we were their own. We loved to go there for a lot of reasons, but one was because Eshie fixed us wonderful frozen sherbert when we would come and visit. Both Ann and I remember the time she sneaked tapioca into our bowls instead, and we tried desperately to eat it as we had been told NEVER to hurt Eshie's feelings. We ate a spoonful or two, then whined to Esh that we were just so full that we couldn't eat another bite. Suspecting the truth, she said, "That's too bad. I was hoping you could eat a little of this sherbert." And we said we would love to, and we dived in and gobbled up a whole bowl of sherbert. Neither Ann nor I can stand tapioca to this day.

Eshie was the only one we ever knew who cut off the crust from the store-bought "light" bread, and she would make us several sandwiches on this de-crusted bread with a spread that we called "Good Stuff." We loved it and always ate at least two sandwiches apiece. We learned later that the "Good Stuff" was nothing but Miracle Whip, but the cut-off crusts made it very special. We never had Miracle Whip out on the farm anyway, as it required refrigeration, and that made it a real treat.

    Also Eddyville was the only place in the county that had a movie theatre, and many was the afternoon that Ann and I sat glued to our seats watching Gene Autry ride off into the sunset on his faithful horse, Champion. We sometimes saw the Lone Ranger and Tonto, and serials that kept us coming back for more as often as we could. These westerns were a primary cause of us playing "Cowboys and Indians" constantly at home. I'm sure, and for our desperate longing to have cowboy suits, guns, holsters, and hats. Poor Mama—she finally gave in and bought us the entire outfits one year for Christmas.

The Way We Were

CHAPTER III
THE FOUR OF US

The house that I was born in on August 4th, 1933, was torn down when Barkley Lake took over most of "Old" Eddyville. My sister Ann remembers the night I was born, even though she was only two years and nine months old, because she was not allowed to go into Mama and Daddy's room and was taken to a neighbor's to spend the night. The next morning, she was brought in to see the new baby, and when she was held up to look she said with disappointment, "Oh, that's just Joe-baby," mistaking me for the boy down the street. Doctor Moseley, who was standing by, said, "That will be her name." And from that day forward he never called me anything else. Lucky for me, my parents decided to keep the "Jo," but to change the "baby" to "Nell" to honor Mama's aunt. When I was in the seventh grade just before we moved to Louisville, some classmates started calling me Nellie, which I couldn't stand—so I changed the spelling of my name to Jonelle, and took the new name with me.

I was the youngest on either side of the family, and was constantly having to prove that I could take my place with the best of them, and that I wasn't a baby. If anyone double-dog-dared me to do anything, you could consider it done. Whether it was jumping from a high hayloft, or swinging across a raging creek on a grapevine, it was a done deal. Ann remembers that I would say, "I'll do it, I'll do it, I've done it!!!" when swinging across the creek. Then Jack, who was one year older than I, would get real red in the face and say, "Ann, we've gotta do it, we've gotta do it." And I would be standing on the other side of the creek, grinning. It wasn't that I wasn't afraid. It was just that I preferred a broken arm or deep laceration to the taunt of being called a "scaredy-cat" or a "baby".

My sister was always just like I wanted to be. Ann was much prettier than I, with her deep auburn hair and bright blue eyes. She loved excitement, never seemed to lose control of a situation, and was fiercely independent from the beginning. She always knew what to say to adults, and she was popular with her peers from early childhood. From the time any of us can remember, her clothes and appearance mattered greatly to her. I can't remember a time that I didn't want to be like Ann.

My father, John R. Jones, was my mentor for as long as I can remember. He was totally honest and fair in any situation, whether it benefitted him or not did not influence his decision in any way. He tried to teach us to "do the right thing," and said that we would never be sorry if we did. He was overprotective of us - so was Mama - but that was only because he cared so much for us. I guess the thing that was most impressive about my Daddy was the enormous love that he carried for his entire family. That was made clear to me by the story that he told me of when he was a young boy of twelve. He went out to the front yard (Grandmother always called that part of the yard "the park") and hid behind an old stump out there to pray. He asked God to end the world before any of his sisters or his brother left home, because he thought he just could not bear to let any one of them go.

Daddy was born on December 7th, 1896, in Lyon County, just a few miles from the house that we would come to know as "Grandmother's house." He was the first son, with older sisters Clara, Ileen, and Maude. Porter, the youngest, was the only one born in Grandmother's house. Just out of school, Daddy went to Fairview to teach, where one of his students in the eighth grade was named Mary Clift. He loved teaching, and considered this his finest profession, even though he had several other occupations during his lifetime and would not return to teaching when he came back from his voluntary stint in the army of the first World War. Returning to Lyon County after his war duty in France, he was asked to come to the penitentiary to be Chief Clerk. He was still in this job when he married Mary in January of 1930. The politics of the day would not allow him to stay in this position when the Democrats were elected in 1933, and he was dismissed from his job at this time. By that date, he had a wife and two children—and the Depression was still in full swing. From all this, I find it easy to understand his lifelong tendency to constantly worry about money.

In January, 1934, my Grandfather Clift (we called him Daddy Clift) died, and left his wife, Nannie, to take care of their farm. It was a natural thing for us to move out there for Daddy to help Mom Clift until different arrangements could be made. We stayed there through 1935, at which time Grandfather Jones asked him to come home to take care of the farm for him. There was a small house on this farm that we could have, and this is the first first house that I remember calling "home".

By far and away the hardest blow my Daddy suffered during these years was the death of his favorite sister, Maude. She had been the light of his life up until he had a family of his own. She died at age forty-two in the spring of 1937, and her husband Bernie came with his two young sons, Hugh Glenn and Jack, to live with Grandmother and Grandfather. This provided Grandfather with another farm manager, so in 1938, Daddy bought a farm in the Fairview area from Mama's brother and sisters, built a house, and this is where we lived until 1945. During World War II, he worked as the head of the Lyon County Ration Office, and his ethics demanded that his family get the smallest number of stamps for sugar, shoes, meat, coal, oil, and gas that we could survive on. From here, he went to his Internal Revenue Service job in Louisville.

Ann remembers a story about Daddy that showed his devotion to Grandmother. When we lived in the little house, "Daddy did such a kind thing. He wanted a "Courier-Journal". That shows what kind of person he was that he wanted a newspaper every day, even in those conditions. But instead of having it delivered to us, he had it delivered to Grandmother so she could read the paper and he would walk up there and get it. He was always very careful to fold it back just right to take to Grandmother in case she hadn't finished with it, and all this was never discussed."

She also remembers when he would walk her to Fairview in her first year, a distance of three miles: "I was scared to death of school and very shy. So, when Daddy saw that I would stand on the sidelines and watch all the other children play, he taught us all how to play 'Bear' and he would play with us. And I think he taught us to play 'Base.' Anyway, Daddy would be the big bear and the kids loved to play with him. So, he'd walk with me many times, and we'd get there early and he'd play with us until the teacher rang the bell. And I didn't know for years later that he did that because he saw that nobody was playing with me."

Daddy died of a heart attack on January 13th, 1969 in Louisville. We took him "home" to be buried in Lyon County at the New Bethel Cemetery in the midst of generations of his ancestors, his father and his sister Maude.

My Mother, Mary Clift Jones, worked really hard all of her long life. She was born on August 25th, 1907, the youngest of four: Estie, Ethel (Esh), White and Mama. She was a happy child, playing mostly with White. They walked to school at Fairview along the road with the other children who would be walking from a greater distance, as the Clifts lived just about one mile from the school. They always looked for horse shoes as they walked, because they thought that would bring them good luck. Church was another big part of her life, as they never missed a Sunday or a Wednesday night. Even though they were Baptists, they went to the Fairview Methodist Church because of the location—Fairview was the only Church in walking distance. Mama sang in the choir and Estie taught Sunday School every Sunday, but the traveling preacher came only once a month.

When she finished the eight grades at Fairview, she wanted to desperately to go to business school. But Daddy Clift thought that was not a good thing for a lady to do, so she stayed on the farm, learned to drive his car, and drove him around the county wherever he needed to go.

She married Daddy when she was twenty-two, and her life as a wife and mother began. I remember Mama when we were children as always having time for us. She would be doing her chores, which included canning, cleaning, washing and ironing clothes, planting a garden, making our clothes, cooking meals, taking care of the chickens, milking the cows, and a hundred more that I can't think of right now, and she would still find time to read to us. Especially when we were sick. I remember listening to her read Heidi, chapter by chapter, many times when we had scarlet fever. Another book I remember is A Child's Garden of Verses, which we heard so many times that we had most of the verses memorized. When we were sick, we would pretend that we were the little boy in "The Land of Counterpane." When Maude died and Bernie moved with his boys to Grandmother's, Jack came to our house every single day until we moved to Fairview. Mama looked after him just the same as she did Ann and me, and was so happy to be able to help take care of him as he was only four when his mother died. She had a big old hollow Easter Bunny that was dressed in blue overalls, and she would make us come to her and shut our eyes tight. Then she would shake the rabbit several times, and we would reach under him when we opened our eyes, and there would be a cookie for each of us. We three really did believe he was the 'real' Easter Bunny.

Then she started reading us stories about a little boy named Peter Painter that came in one of her magazines. Jack remembers: "We'd hide our eyes and she would talk funny like she was Peter, and we thought he had really come, and that he'd brought us an apple or a cookie." And one time, an animal had run across our porch leaving tracks in the snow, and then we knew for certain that Peter was real, and that he had left those tracks. She had to try to get Jack out of a tree one day, where he had caught his heel when he fell, and he was hanging upside down fairly high up. He was swinging in the air for some time as she could barely reach him, and he was scared to death. She headed up the 4-H program that Ann and I belonged to for at least one year, and maybe more. It ended up that she would have to make whatever article of clothing we were required to do as a project. Ann and I loved belonging to the 4-H, as we couldn't wait for the meetings, but neither one of us had the patience or the desire to sew.

So, Mama's hours were filled from morning until night, but my childhood memories of her are that she was mostly happy, that she sang a lot, and that she always had time for us. You can't ask for anything more than that.

The Way We Were

Mary and John

Jo and Ann

Ann, Daddy, Jo

The Four of Us

Ann in the plaid skirt

Jo

The Way We Were

CHAPTER IV
THE JONES CLAN

My Grandfather John Jones died in the summer of 1941, just months before the bombing of Pearl Harbor. He had been ill for several years with what we know as Alzheimer's Disease, but in those days it was common to say a person like that had "gone crazy." He scared me when he would stand in his own house in front of a blazing coal fire grate, crying and begging Daddy to take him "home". Daddy would get him in the car and drive up to Fairview, on over to the Eddyville Train Station, and complete the circle to get him back to the house where he would be content again for a little while.

Grandfather was born on November 8th, 1863, in Lyon County, the youngest child of ten born to William and Malinda. From stories told, he was spoiled by his older brothers all his life, even to the extent that his brother Tom gave him the two-hundred-and-forty-acre farm where my Daddy and his siblings grew up. Shortly after the deed was signed, the railroad crossed this farm lengthwise in two places, thus securing John with money enough to live comfortably the rest of his life, if he was careful with it. From this time on, he spent lavishly on his friends, fished and hunted away his days, and generally had a good time, disregarding entirely the concept of saving for a rainy day. Ann remembers the story Daddy told her about the time before he married when he was talking to Grandfather about life insurance: "Daddy was talking to him seriously, discussing beneficiaries. And Grandfather said, 'Now wait a minute, John, let me get this straight. You pay out all this money while you are alive, right? And then if you die, someone else gets that money? That's the most ridiculous idea that I've ever heard of.'"

He was popular with his peers—he was the second Republican ever to be elected Sheriff of Lyon County, a four-year position he acquired in 1917 (the first was his brother Tom).

He was cheerful and friendly to everyone, and would often surprise an uncomplaining Cordie by bringing home a host of friends for a meal on the spur of the moment. Ann remembers times when he could come down the road in his car, honking his horn, inviting one and all to a fish fry if he had been successful on a certain outing. Ann says, "I remember his big fish fries, because I used to get so excited. Grandmother never knew when he would be coming home, and then he would be driving down the road calling out for people to come. And Grandmother would get Aunt Mag, and Mama would go running up, and Aunt Clara, and I guess Aunt Maude until she died. I just remember the feel of it. They would set up big tables, out in the park, and everybody in the neighborhood would come, and Grandfather loved it."

I remember being included along with my cousin, Jack, on only one of these really early morning fishing expeditions, and I was very cold and damp, but thrilled to be there with him. I remember seeing him skin a rabbit in the side yard with dexterity after he had been hunting, and being so impressed that he was that quick and that good, but not wanting to eat rabbit for some time after that.

Jack remembers Grandfather: "He was a hunter. I mean he hunted turkeys, he hunted birds, and was one of the best bird shots that ever was in Lyon County. Grandfather had an order for forty-eight quails for a certain restaurant in Kuttawa, and he had to get them there for dinner (noon) on Saturday. He didn't get to go on Friday, but he got up early on Saturday morning and took his best dog. He said, 'I killed fifty birds, and had forty-eight of them dressed and in Kuttawa by ten o'clock.' In one morning! I remember Grandfather's watermelon patch—we would put them in the creek to get them cool, and we would keep them on the back porch too. They were always out there lined up on the back porch. And could he grow watermelons. And he grew strawberries. He would let people from all over just come into his strawberry patch and pick as many as they wanted."

I think of him with bananas. He usually bought them on the stalk, and gave them to anyone who wanted them.

He loved the game of Rook, and there would be a game going in the room we called the "house" every time four people gathered who knew how to play. He was particularly kind to my mother when she married into the family. He would choose her for his partner, never criticizing her playing, but commanding her to bid every time he couldn't claim it. When he would take a trick, he would smack the card down on the table with a big flourish according to Ann, who would often be under the card table.

He kept a journal for years, stating every entry with the temperature, weather and any birth notices of the county. Jack notes, "One of his all-famous entries was: 'Well, I've been out with (so-and-so) on a turkey hunt between the rivers, and was gone three or four days. Mrs. Jones was out of humor when I got home.'"

After he was ill, he became particularly fond of red Easter eggs. The red eggs were favorites of most of the children as well, and we all cringed when we would see Grandfather coming towards us after the big yearly hunt in his yard. He would take his walking stick and poke it at the red eggs that we had found, and we were all instructed to give any to him that he wanted, so we always had to hand them over.

He was almost seventy-eight years old when he died, and he is buried in the New Bethel Cemetery.

My Grandmother Jones' name was Cordie. Daddy idolized her, and could never find a single fault with her. Ann and I felt the same way. When I asked Ann what she remembered about Grandmother, she was quick to answer: "I remember a lot about Grandmother. She always looked the same to me. She had brilliant blue eyes and her hair was always pulled back in that little knot. And she laughed a lot. I remember her telling her stories. I would try to sit as close as possible to her feet on the floor. Even the older ones, Portia, Hilda and Hugh Glenn, would come in to listen to her stories. She would read them out of McCall's, or some magazine, and she would read us those stories, but she would put her own bit into them. She would change them if she didn't like them.

And I remember taking walks with her when she would look for rocks and tell us about them being Indian stones. We would walk in creek beds, and she had two rock piles that she kept at home. One was for Indian rocks, and one was just interesting shapes, and she never mixed them up.

She used to cook all kinds of greens. She would collect an assortment in her apron with the rocks. Grandmother could mix the most marvelous greens—dandelions, taking stuff off trees, and sometimes mushrooms, and Mama was sure she was going to make a mistake and get deadly stuff and we'd all get poisoned, but she never did."

I guess my own memory of Grandmother is mainly of her telling her stories that sometimes terrified me, but I would grit my teeth and listen to every word. Sometimes they would not have storybook endings, and we always knew that was a possibility, but we listened every chance we got. She had a wonderful voice, and we were mesmerized. I also remember her singing two children's songs—"Froggie Went A-Courtin'" and "Over in the Meadow." We knew the songs but didn't sing with her—we were too engrossed in listening. And I remember her kindness to every human being. At the time we were on the farm, it was just following the depression, and there were a lot of desperate people around. Hobos on the trains that crossed Grandfather's fields were frequent visitors to Grandmother's house, and usually they would be almost starving. She would take them into the kitchen and fix up whatever she could find—the best she had—and let them sit in peace and eat. She never had a threat from them, or a scare, and when the family told her she had to stop doing that because it was dangerous, she did not argue, but neither did she stop. With one hobo, her old dog just had a fit, and began growling and barking at the man.

This made her a little leery of him, so she had him sit outside at a table, and she still brought the best food she could find. She had no fear in her.

Grandmother lived to be one hundred and four years old, living thirty years after Grandfather died. I guess that is why we always considered the house as hers. In her later years, her hearing became impaired, but her mind never did. And we were never sure just how hard of hearing she really was. If someone at the table said a curse word, no matter how far away from her they were sitting, she always heard it and let them have it. In her later years, she could never call the men by the right name, and she would begin, "Porter, I mean John, I mean Hugh Glenn..." and everyone teased her about that. She would laugh at herself as well. She always referred to Grandfather as "Mr. Jones".

Grandmother had help from Aunt Mag, who lived down the road further than we did. I seem to remember a tale about how her people had been slaves to Grandfather's family, and they moved on when they were freed. But a little later they returned, as they had found that life with the Jones family was easier than life without them. That may have been one of Jack's tales, but I always thought it was true, and all of us adored Aunt Mag. Mama said that the only time she could get Ann to stop crying when she was a baby was to give her to Mag. Ann remembers that her head was always wrapped up in a cloth, and she says, "When Aunt Mag got sick, Grandmother stayed with her until she died. I remember Daddy and Bernie were worried about Grandmother, and how to get her away from there, but she stayed there until Aunt Mag died."

Eastertime and Christmastime were the best at Grandmother's, and I will go into those holidays a little more thoroughly later on

The Jones Clan

in another chapter. One thing I loved at her house—there were usually enough people at her meals to fill the big dining room table twice, so she would have the children go first, and the grown-ups follow. This made sense, as the children couldn't wait to get finished eating, and then the grown-ups could take their time, and relax without the children looking over their shoulders and whining about how hungry they were. And there was never any danger of running out of food.

Grandmother died on June 28th, 1973, outliving every one of her children except Ileen. She is buried in New Bethel Cemetery, next to her "Mr. Jones".

Aunt Clara was Daddy's oldest sister, and she was like a second mother to us all. Never one to mince words, she would tell us just what she thought and let us have it if we needed it. She never married, but we always believed that she had been disappointed in love when she was young. Whatever the reason, she lived out her days helping Grandmother run the house, and taking care of all the children. Her favorites, naturally, were Jack and Hugh Glenn, as she had been at home when they were brought there to live in 1937. She could not have loved them more had they been her own. But she was wonderful to us all, and I simply loved it when she would ask me to do something for her such as to go to pick a bucketful of blackberries for her to make pies. I hated the briars and the possibility of snakes, but I felt good knowing she trusted me to do a good job, and I would stay the course until I had picked as many as I could carry.

My sister remembers a time when she and Aunt Clara got into it: "During the time you were in the hospital, Jo, Daddy and I had to go to stay at Grandmother's. Junior (Hooks, a cousin) was there for the summer and that was kinda fun cause

Junior was so nice to me. Well, Daddy wanted to take me with him to see you in the hospital, but I did not want to go back to 'hot' Paducah. So, I stayed there by myself. I had on unionalls, and Junior and I were going to pick some kind of berries in the woods and we were going to make ink. Aunt Clara wanted me to put on my old dirty unionalls, but I refused to do that. I said I wouldn't get any ink on them. Well, Junior and I went off to the woods and made the ink and got it all over my new overalls, and Aunt Clara was so mad. She really let me have it. I was mad at her—just furious at her for being so angry at me. I was embarrassed because she had gotten so mad at me, and I crawled under the chair of that great big old porch furniture that they had, and I refused to come out and go to dinner. And guess what? They all went in and left me! Under the chair—and I didn't know how to come out and get into the dining room. Every single soul got up and went in the house. They were having dinner and I was left! Including Junior—he said he was hungry."

Our other relatives on the Jones side were the Greenes, the Hooks and Uncle Porter's family. Aunt Ileen and Uncle Floyd always lived in Hopkinsville, and Uncle Porter and Aunt Marie lived in Louisville, so I felt like I did not know them nearly as well as I knew the Greenes. I do not remember Aunt Maude, as she died when I was three. Ann tells of the day she passed away: "Aunt Maude was the funniest one. She laughed all the time—Daddy's favorite. She had wonderful blondish hair—it might have been light red—and she had very bright, bright blue eyes. She really liked me. She was always on the porch at Grandmother's when I came home from school. I remember the day she died because that was really a traumatic time. I don't remember who was helping her, but Grandmother could hardly walk, and she was coming down the little sidewalk, and crying, which terrified me. There were two men, Daddy or Uncle Porter or somebody, one on either side of her, holding her up as she walked in. We were around in the back of the house, and all the kids were back there, and I think Melodine (Riley) was with us and Artie Jean (Cook)—there was a whole bunch of us back there, and Aunt Mag was back there with us. She was in the chair by the big old black kettle where she used to do the wash and we were playing back there. Maggie Riley came around the corner and said, 'Jack, your Mamma is dead.' Just like that. Jack was four years old, and he burst into tears and ran for Aunt Mag. She had this great big fat lap, and this big apron, and Jack dived in her lap. I remember her taking the corners of her apron and just folding them around him, and she just held Jack like that for a long time."

Jack and Hugh Glenn were just as close as they could be to us. Hugh Glenn was older, and off in school a lot of the time, but was wonderful to us when he was around. I remember going to plays that he was in, and wanting to go up on the stage and help him out when he got in trouble. He was always laughing and teasing us, but in a good way. He learned to play the guitar, and I loved to hear him play and sing "The Isle of Capri". During World War II, he joined the Navy just out of high school, was transferred to the Marines, and was shipped to the Pacific. He spent the rest of the war in circumstances so unbelievably horrible that he would never speak about it in front of the younger children. Even in those dire surroundings, he took time to send grass skirts to Ann and me, and to answer every single letter that I wrote him. On one of his leaves, he came home for supper and and stayed to teach Ann how to dance—one of her favorite memories. Jack and I looked on and were so embarrassed that we threw biscuits at them as they whirled around the floor until after midnight.

Jack was my soul-mate, as I have stated once before. Whatever mischief I was in, he was there ahead of me. We saw him every day for two or three years when we lived at Grandfather's, and usually it was from dawn til dusk. We shared treats, toys, ideas, games, and whatever else we might come up with. I never once told on Jack, and he never told on me. We were even in the same grade at school. There will be a lot more about Jack in following chapters. We could not have been closer had we been brother and sister.

Uncle Bernie, Jack and Hugh Glenn's father, was great to kids. He drove a 1933 Chevrolet the entire time we were on the farm—actually until 1949—and it had two big spare tires on it, one on each side. He let Jack drive it once when Jack was just about eight, and Jack didn't quite make the corner at Fairview School. I was in the back seat and remember the car shooting up a dirt bank, and Uncle Bernie rolling out of the passenger seat, wide-eyed at what had almost happened.

He kept a loaded shotgun just inside the front hall door after he came to live at Grandfather's, and the entire county knew not to surprise Bernie in the middle of the night. He was fun for children, very often joining in some of our games. When I married and joined the Catholic Church, he was the one who stood up for me when all the others were teasing me about driving all the way to Dawson Springs to go to Mass. He was my friend.

We didn't get to Hopkinsville very often—it seemed like a hundred miles away—but when we did go, we had a great time. We went there to the Hooks' house for Easter one year that I remember vividly. The eggs had been hidden so well that Jack and I were not finding many, and the adults were competing against us for them as well as all the older children. All of a sudden Uncle Floyd started standing near hiding places and crowing like a rooster. Jack and I would tear over, and sure enough, there would be an egg.

Aunt Ileen was a good cook, and she prepared the same kind of food that we ate at Grandmother's house. In other words, a feast. Ann has this to say about them: "I loved Aunt Ileen, but she had a family and she was way off in Hopkinsville, and I didn't see as much of her. It was such a treat to go to Hopkinsville. I remember going to that big porch that wrapped around the house. And they seemed to have so many kids. They only had four, but it seemed like such a huge family."

Uncle Floyd was funny, but he had a favorite "trick" that scared us to death. He would stand flat on his feet and fall straight forward until his face seemed inches off the floor, then he would spring back up in time to enjoy the astonished looks of all the ladies, particularly Mama, who never failed to let out a loud scream as he was going down.

Of the four Hooks children, we knew Junior the best because of the summers that he spent on Grandfather's farm. He had infinite patience with us, never yelled at us, and taught us wonderful things to know—which berries to use to make ink, how to build a lean-to in the woods, or how to tie good knots. We thought he knew all there was to know. And he would join in all our games anytime we asked him. He was a quiet child, and helpful to Grandmother and Aunt Clara.

Anna Faye came one summer that I can remember, and she mostly wanted to read books and to talk to Grandmother and Aunt Clara. She and Ann had some good times, and I think they spent a great deal of time and effort trying to get away from

Jack and me.

Portia and Hilda were considerably older than we were—at least in a child's eye—and the only time we were really with them was during the stories that Grandmother told. It must have pleased Grandmother enormously that they enjoyed the stories so much, even as they grew older.

Daddy's only brother, Porter, his wife (Marie) and son (John Marvin) weren't around often when we were growing up either, as they lived away during the time I can remember. One story that Daddy loved to tell about Uncle Porter took place when he was a boy. Uncle Porter had climbed to the top of a very tall tree, and was swinging back and forth with the breeze. All of a sudden his footing gave way, and he started crashing down through the tree branches. Very religious even back then, he screamed out, "HOLD ON TO THE LORD!!!" To which practical Daddy yelled back, "YOU IDIOT!!! YOU'D BETTER HOLD ONTO A LIMB!!!" Whereupon Porter grabbed onto one of the very lowest branches and swung himself breathlessly to the ground, scared to death, but unhurt. Daddy took the credit for saving his life.

The Jones Clan

Back Row: Mary (holding Ann), Porter, Marie, Maude, Grandfather, Grandmother, Portia, Clara, Ileen

Front Row: John Marvin, John, Junior, Hugh Glenn, Bernie, Hilda, and Anna Faye (Jack and Jo weren't born yet), Uncle Floyd must have been making the picture, and it is in Grandmother's "Park".

The Way We Were

The Hollow

Grandmother's House

The Jones Clan

Jo, Hugh Glenn, Jack

Grandmother and Aunt Clara

Grandfather, Grandmother,
Aunt Clara, Ann and Jo

The Way We Were

CHAPTER V

THE CLIFT FAMILY

I never knew my grandfather on my Mother's side, as he died when I was about six months old. Stephen Wesley Clift, the second of twelve children belonging to Josiah Robert and Sarah Melinda, was born on Christmas Day, 1862. His mother planted a tree in the yard for each of her children when they were born, and knowing this may have contributed somewhat to his great love of trees, flowers, and all living things.

As a child, he and his brothers drove turkeys to Princeton to sell, and, as that was a far distance, they had to get going very early in the mornings. According to my mother, he set up a saw mill with Nannie's father, Fodie, on the father's farm when he was a young man, and that is where he met his bride to be. They married in Fodie's house in 1892, when he was thirty and she was eighteen. They had six children, two of whom died in infancy. The house they lived in had started out as a log cabin down in one of the fields of the farm, but they brought it up to the road (called The Varmint Trace), and added several rooms onto it. The log part was just the kitchen and the main room of the house that I remember.

Mama remembers him as being very tall and thin, exceedingly gentle and kind. He would often walk in the woods with the children and tell them the names of the trees and flowers. He was quiet and unpretentious, and utterly uncompromising about honesty. He was proud that his only son was able to study hard and become a lawyer.

Ann says of him, "I remember him a little bit. He had a beard or mustache and he was thin. He had high cheek bones. He would wear a hat, a straw-hat kind of thing. I remember him sitting in a rocker. I remember getting on a horse with him because I remember being scared. And I know he rode me in front of him. I can remember holding on to the horn because he told me to. And I guess he had his arm around my waist—he must have—but I remember not feeling too secure up there. I remember the night he died, because there was a lot going on at Mom Clift's, and people were swarming around and were so upset. I had my tricycle and I remember riding it through all these legs and feet, and riding into the kitchen and turning around and riding back. There was just something in the air and that is why I haven't forgotten it." He died of pneumonia in January, 1934, at the age of seventy-two, and is buried in the New Bethel Cemetery.

Nannie White, Mom Clift to us, was born on Puget Sound on May 15th, 1874, which at that time was in Washington Territory as Washington had not yet become a state. Her mother and father, Charles Richard (Fodie) and Annie, had gone west in a covered wagon to search for gold. Before Mom was two, Fodie's father sent for them to come home to help with the farm, and the long trek back across the country began. All four of Mom's siblings were born in Lyon County. Annie was sickly and died when Nannie was 14-years-old, and a lifetime of hard work began for the young girl.

The Clift Family

In 1982, I wrote of Mom Clift: "I remember her quite distinctly as she was during the years 1938-1945. She was tall and thin, big boned, with large hands still capable of doing man's work. She pulled her grey hair severely back from her face to a big bun on the back of her head. She went everywhere in a trot, unable to walk slowly. She was highly moral, and reluctant ever to speak ill of anyone. She was a great cook—I remember her chicken gravy and her fried apple pies best.

She was a doer, not a thinker. I never knew her to read a book except the Bible. She planted a huge garden every year, and canned enough to last the winter. She kept the jars stored on shelves down in the cellar under the smoke house, and there was the most wonderful smell down there when we would go to get a jar of something for her. One of my favorite memories of Mom was when we were sitting on her front porch, after she was over ninety. The preacher came by to see her and when he left, she said 'poor Brother Smith, he's completely senile, and he is only eighty-seven.' She was serious, and we howled with laughter."

Ann remembers: "Mom Clift? I remember her strength, but I don't remember her body being very strong. I think her shoulders were rather narrow. She always held her head very high, and she laughed a lot too. And I remember her opening the chest of drawers and she would always shove it closed with her hip or leg, she never pushed it. That's where she kept the box of candy that Uncle White sent her for Valentine's. When we would go—what a decision to make—because we got only one piece of candy. If we made a mistake, you couldn't put it back and take another. I remember the smell of those chocolates when she would take it out of the drawer and we got one chance.

Mom would always be fussing around in the kitchen. I do remember the fact that both she and Grandmother would cover the table with a tablecloth, and they left sugar and spoons, and jam, and always tea cakes on the table. I would reach under the tablecloth at Mom's and I'd sneak a tea cake, but I was afraid to do that at Grandmother's.

The thing I liked to do best was to stand on the stool and watch her (Mom) clean a chicken. I used to watch her wring the necks, and the chicken would flop around her a couple of seconds after the head was off—that was the thing that impressed me the most. And then she would scald them, and no matter how many times she did it, I never got tired watching. And then she would pluck out all the feathers. And the thing I think I remember the best, was cleaning the gizzard. I used to love that. She showed me how you cut it, and when you opened it, it was all full of sand. She would clean the sand off the gizzard, and I thought that was just marvelous."

Mom lived by herself in the same house she and Daddy Clift fixed up together until just a couple of weeks before she died at age ninety-one in 1965.

Estie, Mama's oldest sister, went to Bowling Green to study teaching when she was a young girl, and was my teacher when I was in the seventh grade at Fairview. She was teaching six grades by herself, which at that time was first through fourth grades, plus two in the upper grades. They had instigated a most foolish method in trying to cut down on the duties for a teacher who had to take care of all eight grades. One year they would have the first through fourth, plus the fifth and seventh. The next year, it would be the first four, plus the sixth and eighth. Lucky for Ann, Jack and me, we happened to be with the group that went right on through. The class behind us and ahead of us had to go to the first four, then sixth, fifth, seventh, and finally graduate from the eighth. I can't imagine how anyone who went through in this hopscotch method could grasp what they were doing well enough to succeed in the following high school years. Anyway, Estie was a really good teacher, and she had a wonderful sense of humor, which I guess carried her through those overworked, stressful days.

Estie was married to Charlie Beck, an uncle that I loved dearly. I never heard him raise his voice and he had a good word to say about anybody we were talking about. He farmed in my early days, but I guess during the war he took a job in town. He used to bring Estie and their daughter, Mary Katherine (when she wasn't in school) to our house when he went to work, and pick them up at the end of the day. Most of these days we would walk down to Mom Clift's to spend the day with her. Mary Katherine was extremely smart in school, and loved to read. She frequently entered contests, and she was often a winner. She was older than I but always had time for me when I needed it.

The only thing I have to add about Esh and Chester is that they always drove a nice new car, and riding in a car with a new-like smell was a constant pleasure to Ann and me, even though we were told never to put our shoes up on the seat. They took us with them to Princeton often, and to Paducah every great now and then. Ann remembers, "And then it was always a big deal, which they did many times, to take us to Paducah. That was the big day. We would ride the elevator up in the 10-story building. I remember one day we just got on the elevator—I don't know why they would have left us by ourselves—Mama must have been going to some doctor or something. We rode up and down on the elevator all afternoon. We never got off it.

We just pushed the buttons and would ride up and down with whoever got on, and we were happy just riding up and down."

Mama's only brother, White, was considered the success of the family. When he was a child, he never worked hard and could always be seen taking a book under his arm when he was sent out into a field to do a job. Mama remembers, "He read all the time. He went to Kuttawa High School, then took a correspondence course on law, and went to law school in Memphis. He took the bar at twenty years old because of his high standings. A newspaper article at that time said he was the youngest lawyer in the south. He went to Oklahoma to handle oil law, and loved it out there from the very beginning."

He and his family—wife Ruth and daughter Mary Ruth—would come to visit Mom Clift for a week or ten days every year of my childhood, and this was an event that rivaled Christmas and Easter in our lives, so it has been written about in detail in the chapter titled "Special Times".

The Clift Family

Nannie and Stephen

Mom Clift's Home

The Way We Were

Charles Richard White, "Fodie"
Mom Clift's Father

The Clift Family

Stephen Clift (Daddy Clift)

The Way We Were

Jo, Nannie, Ann
Notice the boots

Ann, Jo, Mary Katherine, Mary Ruth

The Clift Family

Uncle Charlie Beck with Mary Katherine

The Way We Were

CHAPTER VI

DEAR OLD GOLDEN RULE DAYS

There are so many memories about our days at Fairview school that I doubt I can get them all in, but I'm willing to try. Fairview was the elementary school where Mama and Daddy had gone to school and Daddy had taught there before he went into the service. It was the school that Ann and Jack attended through the eighth grade and graduated from, going on to Kuttawa High School. It was my school until we moved to Louisville following my seventh year. It consisted of one huge room (it seemed huge to me at that time, it probably wasn't that big) that had accordion-like doors in the middle that could be closed if we were lucky enough to have two teachers at one time. There was one pot-bellied stove in each of these sides and windows along one entire side of the building. Blackboards stretched along two sides of the lower grades' room and along one side of the 'upper' room, with an all-important stage on the east side of this room. We had a cistern for our water and an outhouse for our other needs.

The school year started in July and was completed in January, at which time we were excused until the following July. I always thought this schedule was put in place so the children could be at home to help during the busy spring months that always went along with farming. But Jack says it was because we had just those two stoves to keep us warm, and it would have been impossible for them to do the job during the bitter winter months. Maybe it was for both reasons. Our day began at eight o'clock sharp and lasted until four. We had two recesses at ten and two, with an hour off for lunch. This made for an incredibly long day for small children, considering the fact that most of them had to walk miles to get to the school house. Our house at Grandfather's was three miles from the school, which Ann had to walk for a little more than two years, and I had to walk for three months when I was mostly just five years old. When we moved to the Fairview area, we were in sight of the school.

Ann remembers the long walk: "We got to school at eight o'clock, left at four, and I had homework. It was a very long, long, long, day. And Daddy paid James Grubbs—I think it was one dollar a week, or maybe it was fifty cents—to carry my books and my lunch basket. I would be so tired that I would run ahead around a curve and sit down to wait for the others to catch up with me."

Jack adds: "I don't see how Ann kept up with James and Golda (Grubbs). The way they walked. I can see them now coming down that hollow. They were the only three coming that far, Ann would be in the middle, and James on one side and Golda on the other, and how Ann kept up with them, I don't know. Sometimes Ann would stop there at Grandmother's. James would have her lunch box, and maybe her books and whatever, and they wouldn't even slow up when she left them—she would have to get her things on the run. I can just see her reaching up to grab them. And how that kid kept up with them, I don't know. They were great big kids."

Ann also recalls a time when she rode a horse to school: "Then there was this horse who was so pretty and young—Charlie—that I got to ride to school sometimes. The second year I went I guess, and Jack went with me. Daddy still walked with us and it was so nice not having to make that long, long walk. We took turns riding in the saddle, with the other riding behind. That morning, we were at the rocky part; I guess when you went up Rocky Hill as you were coming out of the hollow. I know there were rocks and I was not holding on to Jack like I was supposed to be, and Charlie was a right spry horse. I had turned around to look at somebody in back of me, and Jack kicked Charlie to make him go faster. Charlie jumped out from under me, and I fell off, and the rocks cut my face. Daddy took me to the doctor, but I don't think there were any stitches, as I don't think I ever had any stitches. But that was the end of me riding the horse, because Daddy said I could ruin my face forever. It is a wonder we ever grew up! So that was a sad day when I couldn't ride the horse anymore."

Jack rode to school often after we moved up to Fairview, and he would hitch his mare there in the back of the school. He remembers, "I'd usually tie her up at the tree just to the left of the cistern. If the weather was bad, I'd take her over and put her in your all's barn. Joe Millikan rode a pony almost every day, I'd ride the mare, and James Lester Durroh drove the little buggy and would haul all the kids from down his road. It had sort of a trunk bed in it, and that little buggy would be covered up with kids."

Ann also remembers being terrified on the first day of school: "Well, the first day of school, Daddy went with me. I knew how to add and subtract a little and how to diagram a sentence. I knew how to read, and I knew how to write a little bit cause Daddy had taught us all that. I went into a state of panic on the first day 'cause I started in the second grade, as you did, Jo. I was scared of the teacher, Ms. Cochran, scared that I was going to get whipped. The first thing she did was ask you to write your name and address and I didn't know how to write the address or something, and I went into a state of panic. Suddenly Daddy appeared and he wrote it out for me. He came to my desk and he wrote it out for me."

Ann asks, "Do you remember the night when I had to memorize the poem about the flea and the little mosquito and the turtle that 'snapped at the flea and he snapped at the mosquito and he snapped at me...he caught the something, he caught the flea, he caught the mosquito, but he didn't catch me!' Well, I simply could not get it. I don't remember how old I was, but I was in school and Daddy was impatient and my mind was just blocked. Jo, you were sitting at the table watching this whole scene going on, and suddenly you opened up your mouth and said, 'I know it!' And you did, without missing a word. That was just terrible. I wanted to kill you."

The memories of Ann go on and on, and I love every one of them. If the reader will bear with me, I don't want to leave a single one out that she put on my tape. She remembers the fifth grade: "We were studying Columbus, and it was one of the worst times of my life. I raised my hand and said could we please have a test on Columbus 'cause I loved Columbus. I knew everything about Columbus. Well, we had the test and nobody would speak to me for four days, not even Wanda

Lee, who was my best friend. And I remember going down to Kuttawa Springs—Mama made us go, and I always loved to go, but it was a Sunday afternoon and I knew my friends would all be there and nobody would talk to me or play with me. Finally, Wanda came over and she laid me out, but then she played with me. And we had a play, and all the cast were boys except me, and I got to be Columbus. I wore my little white pants and a little white shirt, and some blue cape of some sort.

I remember being in other plays. I was never afraid of getting up, not afraid at all, and I don't know what grade I was in, maybe fourth grade—and we were doing a PTA play. I had memorized "The Last Leaf" and I stood up and suddenly I had no breath, and I went *gasp* The last leaf upon the tree... *gasp* The last leaf upon the tree *gasp*... and ever since then I've been scared to death of getting up in front of people. It was awful.

We used to have spelling bees and arithmetic matches; I think they called them. At any rate, as we were called up, the person coming up could say what kind of math they wanted. We would face out and the teacher would say 'Turn around'—we would write the whole problem down, and then turn around and face out. Then she would say, 'Ready, set, go!' and we would turn around and work it, and the first one that got through with the right answer won it and the other one had to sit down. I had to set a couple of people down, and felt that I was doing really well when she called you up to challenge me. You had this big grin on your face and you said, 'long addition', knowing full well that subtraction was my long suit. And when I couldn't do it as fast, you set me down. You had a big cat-like grin on your face.

The Way We Were

Do you remember in the election when we had Wendell Wilkie running, Jo? The posters were Mama's and Daddy's—they always had posters because they were the only Republicans in Lyon County, and we were the only children of Republicans in the school. And I remember swearing that when I grew up, I was going to be a Democrat for the sake of my children. Because it was so awful. In the afternoons, you and I went around on your bicycle—on one bicycle—and our job was to hammer all these big Wendell Wilkie posters up. Then the next day they would all be torn down, so we would go back and we would hammer them up again. We couldn't get them all up, so we made the guitars and stuff out of the ones left over and we would stand on the front porch and sing with these guitars. And who was it…down at Mom Clift's that said they heard us? That next morning our teacher, Ms. Bradshaw, made us say The Pledge of Allegiance to the flag, and then we always said a Bible verse—I said 'Jesus wept' many times, any time I hadn't memorized a new one for the day. I was so mortified.

Then I remember Mama and Daddy were always afraid that I would fall in the cistern at school, and I was forbidden to go near it. Well, the biggest thing that happened at school one day was that somebody was dipping in the bucket for a drink and their hat fell in the cistern. So we all went up to take a peek at the hat in the cistern, including me. When we got home I was telling Mama and Daddy about it, and Detective Daddy said, 'How do you know what the hat looked like in the cistern?' Then it turned out that I had leaned over and looked at the hat. I can't remember what happened about this, but it was just awful."

Jack recalls, "Do you remember the lunch cabinet we had there? Old Johnny Glass built it. It had shelves in it, and everybody put their sack lunches in it. It had doors on it just like a cabinet, but what I'm saying, is why in July and August when we set those bologna sandwiches in there, why they didn't spoil before dinner (lunch). Water's all we had to drink, and I brought a tin cup that opened up like an accordion. My own personal cup."

Ann remembers when she was in the fourth or fifth grade, the school was so poor that the government—under some Roosevelt program—sent us gallon jars of peanut butter. She says, "And it would have oil on the top, and I got to help stir the oil into the peanut butter. They sent us quart cans of grapefruit juice, and that was the first time I had ever tasted grapefruit juice. They didn't give it to every school—it was just for the poor schools, and we qualified."

Ann remembers: "We did plays and poems, and we did things for the PTA. We had some kind of program and Jo, they got you to stand up and sing "The Bear Went Over the Mountain", and I sang "At the Cross." You stood up at the blackboard and the whole time you sang, you turned around and turned your head up looking at the blackboard. It was hysterical. You were very young, you must have been about five, and I was no longer scared at school anymore.

"In the third grade, Mama bought me these horrible black patent leather shoes, and they were cheap. I can just see them. They had a big wide strap and a set of buckles, and I cannot remember the socks Mama made me wear with them, but they were beige knee socks that came up under my dress and Artie Jean said, 'You look just like George Washington.' So, Mama and I had a fight every morning because I didn't want to wear those shoes to school again.

Fourth grade was when I began to get a little wild, thank goodness. It was about time. I had been scared to death the first part of my life. I sort of did know my American history and we had a history test every single day. We would have to read a chapter every night and then be tested on it the next day. There would be about ten questions, and if you didn't pass it, you had to stay in at recess and you had to study and you had to retake the test until you got a hundred. That was really tough. But you did learn your history—these were essay questions. Well, I had not studied one time, and I leaned across and said, I think to Wanda, 'Who is Arron Burr?,' and she whispered, 'I think a traitor.' And I wrote this long thing about how he traded stuff with the Indians, and the Indians gave him furs and beads. I had to stay in recess and humiliate myself by having to write all over the blackboard, 'I will never cheat again.'"

One of Jack's memories has to do with the Johnson family, who lived just in back of our house. That family consisted of Charlie and Martha, and their three children, Billy, Bobby and Archie, who was a baby. Daddy had given a small plot of land to these people with a very small house on it because he felt sorry for them. Charlie was a tenant farmer who had nothing at all, yet they would have parties where they drank beer and got sort of wild. We were never allowed to go near the place. One of my clearest memories is about Bobby, who was a couple of years younger than I. We never wore our shoes, because we went barefoot as long in the fall as we could bear it and came out of our shoes at the first sign of spring. I normally wore Ann's hand-me-downs, especially during the war when shoes were rationed. Well, I had a pair of brown shoes that were still good when I outgrew them, and they looked enough like boys' shoes, so Mama gave them to Martha for Bobby to wear. The first day of school that he wore them, the kids were merciless at their teasing of poor little Bobby because he had on girls' shoes. The worst offender was David Preston, who was one year behind me. He really got bad about the teasing during recess, so I entered into my one and only lifetime out and out fist fight. I knocked the stuffing out of David, and promised to do the same thing to anyone else so stupid as to tease little Bobby any more. The teasing stopped right there.

Jack and I both remember a crisis day at school during the seventh grade when Martha appeared at school and scared us to death. She said that Billy had taken about one hundred dollars out of her pocketbook, and if he had given it to anyone there would they please return it to her as she desperately needed it. Well, it turned out that Billy had been renting Joe Millikan's pony and anybody's bicycle that was brought to school. Jack tells me, "For about three days there I was fixing to make a contract with him, cause I had my bicycle and he was going to pay me two dollars a day to ride it from Fairview down to his house. But I never did get involved and never did get any of the money. Martha came up there and she and Estie got together for a minute, and Martha told her that, you know, she knew what had happened, and Estie made an announcement. She said that anybody that had gotten any of that money, 'We expect it to be given back,' and she got the biggest part of it back. He had paid eighteen dollars to Joe for riding the pony and another boy had a lot involved in it for bicycling. I was fixing to—I thought this was a pretty good deal."

Jack goes on to say, "I'll tell a story about Connie Jones—I'm thinking it was in the fourth grade when they were testing our hearing with a Big Ben pocket watch. They would blindfold you, and the teacher would start up close like this to see how far you could hear. She would start close and then back up. You would hold your hand up, and when you got to where you couldn't hear it, you would drop your hand and this showed how far you could hear it. A Big Ben pocket watch back then could probably be heard twenty or thirty feet—it ticked like a clock. Well, Connie Jones kept saying she could hear it. So the teacher went clear across the room and caught her because she said she could still hear it. That's when she knew Connie was cheating."

One other thing I remember vividly about the schoolhouse, is that at least once or twice, we had a musical group that would come and play in connection with our pound suppers or ice cream suppers that we had to make money for the school. I remember the girl would have on a white outfit and would wear white boots with tassels on them. We all would have killed for a pair of boots like that.

Ann remembers, "Oh, Dixie Lee Belle. I wanted to be Dixie Lee Belle more than anything under the sun. There were two of them, and they always used to tap their heels. I would have given half my life for the accordion. All I remember were the white boots that I never got, but we finally got boots. Boots were the thing. And Wanda Lee got white boots—and Mama got me BROWN!! I don't remember, but I think you had black, and I think those black boots came from Mary Ruth. I think she sent a pair of little black boots and you crammed your feet into them. I think Mama bought my brown ones, but I think that's how you got the black ones."

During the summer months, we had a revival one year at the Fairview Methodist Church, which sat fairly close to the schoolhouse. We were all taken from our classes every morning to the services, whether we wanted to go or not. Ann sang in the choir, and would beg Daddy and Mama to take us every night, which I think they did this one year. At the end of the sermon at every service, there was the call to accept Christ while "Just As I Am" would be sung. Ann remembers the day that she felt the call, and went to the front to sit to wait for the Spirit to come to her. She says, "Louise White was sitting next to me with her arm around my shoulders and I had a hard time standing up. I was waiting for something big to come, much like Paul at Damascus, but it didn't happen. So I waited for a decent length of time and then stood up. I remember seeing sunbeams streaming through the windows, shining on some dust in the air, and I thought that was just beautiful. I have told my girls that I want "Just As I Am" to be played at my funeral as I have never forgotten it. I looked across the aisle and there you were. You had followed me. I was really touched by that."

Fairview School in 1938. Ann is seated to the right of Miss Cochron, Jack is just in front of Ann, and Jo is not in school yet.

My seventh grade class at Fairview
Photograph by Jo

CHAPTER VII
SPECIAL TIMES

Each year there were three really special times in our fairly uneventful lives, and they were Christmas, Easter, and Uncle White's coming. These were celebrated in just about equal fervor. We considered all three as holidays. I remember our Christmases as being rather sparse, yet we always had stockings with an orange, peppermints, and candy in them, and at least one toy each that we had been begging for under the tree. I can remember the feeling of excitement that we would have for weeks before Christmas, even at Fairview.

Ann says of school, "One of the best things was our Christmas program when we had the tree. That tree was so huge for me, and it probably wasn't real big at all. But we drew names—do you remember that? How I loved to draw a name. The kids wanted to give to their boyfriend or girlfriend and they would switch around, but you were supposed to keep it a secret who you had. And you never knew until you got the big present who had your name. Then if somebody kinda liked you and gave you something, an extra present, not the person who had your name, that was so exciting. And I will never forget—Jack Millikan gave me a little box of chocolate covered cherries. I was so excited. It made my Christmas."

We usually celebrated our Christmas at home on Christmas Eve so we could go to Grandmother's early on Christmas Day. One special Christmas, Ann remembers, "Then at Christmastime, we were allowed to take one toy to Grandmother's. We didn't get many so it wasn't a hard choice. But we could take one to Grandmother's and I remember the year we got the cowboy suits. We had wanted them so badly because we always played cowboy. Oh, did I want that cowboy suit, and I walked down and looked at the tree. There was no big hat on the tree, so I knew we didn't have the cowboy suits. Well we did, but you should have seen the cheapie! The CHEAP cowboy suit!! It was thin gauze, no—thick gauze—and it was a mustardy yellow color, which was okay, but it was the hat. The hat was made out of the same material, with a wire brim. It was your head pushing through that made it stand up. It had a little vest with it, and we did get guns and holsters, and so we used to play cowboys. It was one of our favorite things, and one of us had to be the bad guy, and the other two, counting Jack, were the good guys, and we would gallop on our horses round and round the house. Tobacco sticks were our horses. We would ride behind the chicken house, but mainly we would ride around the house and under the porches. I think the suits did have plaid shirts. It was the hat that got me. It wasn't nice material, and it was flat until your head fit in it."

Jack adds, "I can't remember a whole lot about Christmases, but I remember one Christmas. You and Ann got the Lone Ranger outfits, the mask—the little black mask. It was the Lone Ranger, the whole deal. And Christmas morning after I got through at

Grandmother's, I came down and you all were out on the porch with your pistols pulled. I said 'Oh, how I would like to have had one of those suits.' I never will forget it."

We loved to get to Grandmother's for the day, because there would be fires burning in both grates, and Grandmother always told her stories to all her grandchildren on Christmas Day. The men usually got up a game of Horseshoes—this was one game that the children did not enter into, at least not when the men were playing. There would be games, outside and inside, all day long. If the weather cooperated, there would have been soft ball, Antony-over, Rook, Marbles, Tag, Hide-and-Seek, Crokinole, and checkers. The meal would be a feast, and you just knew that Grandmother and Aunt Clara had been preparing food for weeks. Every year there was country ham with red-eye gravy, fried chicken with chicken gravy, whipped potatoes, green beans, homemade cornbread and biscuits, fruit salad, pies and cakes, and a table full of other things that I rarely ate. I wanted to 'save room' for the fantastic desserts. Aunt Clara always did the fruit salad, and the thought of it today still makes my mouth water. She also used to bake a gooseberry pie that was delicious. She was a great cook, as was Grandmother.

Easter was celebrated with the same enthusiasm as Christmas, with the entire Jones clan descending on Grandmother's to spend the day. The games would be started early, and of course, the big Easter egg hunt was a yearly added thrill. I remember one year when Jack and I were really young, we thought there weren't enough eggs dyed to be hidden, so a few days ahead, we went out to the chicken house, found about ten extra eggs, dyed them and added them to the basket where the other dyed ones were. We had forgotten that they had to be boiled, and there was absolutely no way to distinguish which had been cooked and which were raw. The thrill of cracking an egg you had found with the idea of eating it on the spot was even a lot greater that year than usual. Not one grown-up there believed Jack and I were innocent—they all thought we had it planned.

The third special time that occurred in our lives every year was the arrival of Uncle White, his wife Ruth, his daughter, Mary Ruth, and usually Snowball, their Spitz dog. They would come driving up from Oklahoma in their huge car, filled to the brim with more clothes than they could possibly wear, and all kinds of Mary Ruth's expensive toys that we would have died for. Mary Ruth's clothes were always of the latest fashion, and we would be holding our breaths to see what she would bring out each year.

Ann says, "Uncle White's coming was the greatest thing. That put excitement in my life. When Uncle White, Ruth and Mary Ruth were coming, that was so exciting. For weeks ahead of time, Mama would go to Mom's and Estie would go, and I don't remember Eshie as much. I do remember the preparation—everything was washed, everything was painted and everything was cleaned from the top to the bottom. And the cooking started. Hams were gotten out and pies and cakes were cooked. They stayed in the two front rooms, the one where the piano was, and the fireplace. So there was a great to-do getting ready for them. Then there would be the great arrival. We would see what toys Mary Ruth would have, and her clothes, and usually she would bring a dog, which we were never allowed to pet. I think she only brought another dog one other time 'cause it was always Snowball, a Spitz.

There was much to do. And then all the big meals there, and Uncle White usually brought fireworks. We never had fireworks for the Fourth of July. We had them for Christmas when we had them. Uncle White brought fireworks we had never seen before. We would all get on the front porch, and he would get out where that maple tree was, and we would hang things from trees. He put on a show, and it seemed that he had hundreds of fireworks. It was very exciting. We would all cheer when they went off. It was very special to have him there on the Fourth of July, because we got the big fireworks show. He brought all sorts of sparklers that we could do, but he did the big stuff."

Ann goes on, "Do you remember when Uncle White took us all to the zoo in Evansville? They left Snowball at Mom's, and she hated that dog. He wasn't used to being treated like a dog. Mom had just left Snowball in the house, and Daddy was there and I think Charlie—Estie and Mary Katherine had gone with us. A terrible storm came up, and Snowball disappeared. Mom knew they would just DIE if anything happened to that dog. So, they looked all over—Daddy looked, and he wasn't mad about Snowball either, Charlie looked—and all the neighbors came to help look, and Mom was yelling and screaming out in the storm for this dog, and they didn't know what they were going to do. Mary Ruth and Ruth were going to DIE over that blasted dog. When they finally gave up and came in, Snowball had hidden under the bed!

Ruth used to say 'I will send you clothes,' and one time she did. I think she always intended to do it but that was the only time she did. Mary Ruth had one ABC dress that was just so nice and it had embroidery on it—it was white, with colored embroidery. I thought it was wonderful. We were all going to a carnival and Mary Ruth wore the ABC dress that night, but Ruth didn't want her going out without an undershirt under the dress. Mary Ruth wouldn't wear an undershirt because 'Ann didn't have to wear one.' So Mama made me wear one. Was I mad. It was the middle of summer no less. Mama made us an ABC dress after they left, but it was out of terrible material. It was not like Mary Ruth's. And then when I was just starting to be a teenager, I was probably 12, she came with probably forty-two plaid skirts, and it was the first year of the Sloppy Joe. Hers were long like they were supposed to be and the bobby socks—and Mama bought me a purple and green flared skirt, but no Sloppy Joe. She got me a short-sleeved sweater. Mary Ruth had all sorts of dickies and she wore makeup that year.

When she was young, she had a pony in Oklahoma City—she didn't even live on a farm. And I wanted a pony more than anything. I told Mary Ruth that I had a pony out in Mom's field—out and out lied. I swore I had a pony and I described him, but she was doubting the whole time.

She said 'I don't believe you' and she called Mama.

Mama said 'ANN!!! What are you talking about? You know you don't have a pony.'

And Esh said 'Mary, why do you say that? Of course Ann has a pony. You just don't want to have to go and get it because it is over in the back field.' So she backed me up.

There was one time when Daddy was literally going to get me a pony when we very young at Mom Clift's. The man brought the pony with a little saddle on it and they put me on the pony. I had ahold of the reins, and Daddy and the man were discussing I guess the price, and the pony wandered off. He went under the clothes line, and it just cleared my head, and Daddy said no pony! Because I could have killed myself on the clothes line. That was one of the saddest days of my life.

I remember once when we were at the cabin at Mom Clift's playing, and something started to chase us. I think it was a pig, and we were all three scared to death and took off running. You and I were very used to fences, and we jumped over—cleared the barbed wire on the top. Mary Ruth got caught in the barbed wire, and there was a big cut in the top of her leg. I remember this great big gash, and there was much to do over it. They went back to Oklahoma City and Uncle White built her a little fence with barbed wire on it so she could learn to climb over the fences at Mom's.

When they would leave, everybody would cry. Mom Clift would start and White would be crying—Ruth didn't cry—and everybody would be lined up just bawling. And the big car would pull out and we would all wave. The summer after you would be sick with colitis, do you remember the big oak tree as you went out the drive, not the one in the yard where we used to try to walk around without touching hands—I mean the split oak tree, or two by the driveway. Well, this time Mary Ruth left you some toys because you had been so sick, and she didn't leave me anything. We had been playing out by that oak tree, and I stood there amidst all the tears hoping that she would not remember about the blue telephone that she had forgotten out by the oak tree. I prayed she wouldn't remember, and the minute that car disappeared, I ran to the big oak tree and got the blue telephone."

One other yearly entertainment that we loved, but not quite on the level of 'The Big Three', was the coming of Bisbee's. This traveling show would set up a tent in Kuttawa in a big old lot behind Maddox's store. They would stay six nights, Monday through Saturdays, and Ann and I would cry and beg to go every night. You could buy little boxes of treats when you went in the door that had prizes in them, and one box would have the stub that entitled you to the BIG prize. We cried for the boxes every time we went, but we never won the BIG prize.

Tuesday night was the best night, as that was when The Red-Headed Toby was featured, who was a comedian and the hit of the entire show. Every year Mr. Bisbee would trade his car in when he was in Kuttawa, and in 1936 my Daddy bought Bisbee's car from Mr. Clarence Jones' shop where it had been traded. Daddy drove this great big old black 1935 Chevrolet until 1948. It was a great car.

CHAPTER VIII
THE WAY WE WERE

The days of our young lives were spent in school and studying half the year, with the other half being spent in having a good time along with doing a few chores. The chores I remember were few and far between, yet we were expected to do our part. Daddy had bought Mama a new washing machine which was just a tub on legs that had a washboard and a wringer was attached to the top. The wringer consisted of two rollers spaced close together, and you would run the clothes through this by turning a handle. This pressed most of the water out, and then the clothes would be hung out on the line to dry. Ann helped Mama with the wash while I 'cleaned the house'. I don't remember ironing at home—probably Mama was afraid we'd get burned—but I remember ironing one or two pieces at Mom Clift's. The irons were heavy, with the weight embossed on the iron at the top, either six, seven, or eight pounds. They were kept heating on the stove, and you would grab one iron and press the clothes quickly before it ran out of heat. When it cooled you would put it back on the stove and grab a second iron. Grandmother and Aunt Clara would still wash in a huge old black kettle with a fire under it to heat it, and they stirred the clothes with a broom handle. It would take them all day to do a wash.

I remember helping Mama with the garden. She would go first down a row to be planted with corn or whatever, and she would use the hoe to make the hole in the ground. I could come next with the grain of corn or seed and put it in the hole, and then Ann would follow and cover it up and mash the dirt down. We also had to help gather in the vegetables when they were ready, and I can remember the sheer joy it was to dig down in a hill and find four or five big potatoes and carry them into the house.

Another chore I remember so clearly was when Daddy would bring the hay in from the field and would need us to help him get it into the hayloft of the barn. He would have it in a wagon, and he would drive it down to the front of the barn. There was a big forklift that had only two tongs, and it had a rope attached to it that went up to pulleys in the top of the hayloft, across the barn, out an opening in the back, and down to the back lot. There the rope would be tied onto one of our mules. Ann and I would be standing with the mule, ready to walk him to the very back of the lot when Daddy called out that he had jammed some hay onto the forklift. The movement of the mule with the rope would pull the forklift up to the loft, and someone up there would pull the hay off. Then the person in the loft would let the forklift back down to Daddy and Ann and I would have walked the mule back to the barn to wait for the next call. This was a very slow but sure method of getting the hay into the barn for wintertime feeding.

Ann remembers helping at Mom Clift's: "We would climb up on a ladder with peaches or apples. Mom would spread out cloths on the slanted roofs of the buildings and we would put out the fruit. They stayed there for a long time, and then we would go and collect them, and that's what she would make her pies with. She kept her regular apples in the top part of the cellar, which was in the smokehouse. The smokehouse was there at the back porch. On the first floor there was the grinder where we used to grind corn for the chickens. Then you went down the steps, straight, straight down steps into the cellar. We were told that apples couldn't touch each other or they would rot. You couldn't do a bag of apples, you had to lay them all out. And then you could eat those all winter.

I also remember helping Mom to churn butter. We would sit on the back porch next to the cistern and lift and lower the handle of the churn for what seemed hours before the butter would be made. I always got to go first as that is when the churning was easy."

Ann remembers another chore: "Our house was in the middle of a field, it wasn't even a lawn, and it was our job to keep that acreage mowed with a push mower. We would get tired pushing, and then we would tie the mower to your bicycle and one of us would pedal the bicycle and the other one would guide the mower. That didn't help very much. We actually mowed almost every day. Another thing we used to do during that time was to sit on the bank by the highway when they would be smoking tobacco in the barns. We didn't have tobacco, but barns would be around us that did and we would get hysterical because car after car would stop and tell us that the barns were on fire."

She recalls helping at home: "I remember helping Daddy build fences. He would stretch the wire because I couldn't do that. But as soon as he got the handle on the wire, I could hold it while he hammered it in. I remember him telling me that I saved him so much money because he had to pay Ray Arnold a dollar a day to help him do the things he couldn't do by himself. And one time Daddy had to fertilize as it was going to rain or he hadn't gotten the field done, and it was late in the afternoon. I remember telling him that I could drive the wagon and he could fertilize from the back of the wagon. He wasn't sure I could do it, but you and Daddy and I went over to the field. I got up on the driver's side, and we had taken our dolls with us, and I drove the wagon. I guess I did fairly well because Daddy was able to get it done, but poor Betty Lou (doll) fell off the wagon, and the wagon rolled over her and broke her arm. I was destroyed."

We each had three dolls, and Ann remembers that hers were Betty Lou, Martha Ann, and Sonny. Mine were Betty Jean, Snow White and Bobby. When I was about seven or eight, Ann and I started playing like I was a little kid named Bobby and she was my Aunt Martha who I lived with. I started talking a funny talk, perfected it, and spoke only in this language whenever we were playing Bobby and Martha. Ann could understand what I was saying, but she never learned to speak it. I knew how to say any word that was in the English language, but I can't for the life of me remember the method I used. We played that way for a long time.

Other games we would play were the ones I have talked about that would be going on at Grandmother's or at school.

Ann tells, "Oh, I would get so scared at Grandmother's because I was little, and we would chase around the cars that were parked and turn and run. I just hated that, even watching it. And then Antony-over. You would throw the ball over the roof over the kitchen and smokehouse, and if you caught it, you could run around and someway you got somebody else on your side. I know. You ran around and tried to hit somebody with the ball. If you missed it when it came over the roof, you had to just throw it back over. You tried to fool the other side—you could yell something, but you couldn't yell "Antony-over". But you could fool them and come tearing around the house with the ball. And I sometimes remember Daddy and Uncle Bernie playing, but not much, but I remember Hugh Glenn and Junior playing a lot. We were so little to try to throw that ball over."

She remembers, "We had corn cob fights and that hurt. You would throw corn cobs and try to hit people in the stable, and the haylofts. It is a wonder that dust didn't kill us. We'd play cops and robbers there, hiding behind the hay. And I remember particularly the Horseshoe games. The men did that. We would try sometimes, but not when the men were playing. They loved pitching the Horseshoes and baseball. And we would race to the big sycamore tree. Do you remember that? You could always beat Jack and me in a race."

Jack remembers, "I know we played marbles. And the years you all lived down below Grandmother's, 'course I came every day. Every day, I mean, you know. And do you remember how the old smokehouse set up on the hill? We would put on shows, coming out from behind the smokehouse. We would be Gene Autry, or some other star, and you'd be the star in one and Ann and I would sit on the ground and watch. Then Ann or I would go next. We'd wear our guns, and when you all had the outfits, we'd wear them."

Ann remembers when the three of us would play FBI and spy on the Johnsons who lived down in back of us. She says, "The field was grown up in grass and Jack really got scared to death. And I know none of us—certainly not Jack—ever went as close to that house as we said we did. But two of us would stay back in the chicken house, which was our headquarters. Not all three ever went in case we didn't come back. We would crawl on our stomachs in that tall grass and lie there and listen to everything they would say—usually on Sundays because that was when they would have their parties. Then we would crawl back and embellish what we had heard. We would then all have a session on what we thought we should do about it. But I'm sure Jack never got as close as he said he did. I'm sure he was scared to death."

Jack was also 'scared to death' when he and I climbed up on a speeder that had been left on the railroad track.

Ann remembers that day vividly: "We were playing up there, and do you remember speeders? Speeders were what the workers rode on the railroad track. They pushed a handle up and down and that's what made the thing move. The men rode on speeders to wherever they had to work on the track. One day there was a speeder and no men on it, it was just on the railroad track. So you and Jack and I went over to investigate, and you and Jack thought it would be fun to just take a little ride. Just to pull that thing once and go down the track just a little bit. And I said I was not going to have any part of it because the men would be coming back from lunch or something, and I didn't want to get caught. I tried to stop you, but no way. The two of you climbed on the speeder, and Jack and you gave it a pull and push, and the speeder took off. It started going down the railroad track and you couldn't stop it.

I remember how red Jack's face was. It was absolutely purple. And his eyes were huge, and he was scared to death. I was scared to death too, because here was this terrible situation, but I was so glad that you couldn't stop it. You went maybe twenty yards down the track, and it stopped."

I remember one time when I was scared to death. Ann and I had been sent into the woods to look for a cow that had not come in, and we came upon a black snake. It took off running after me, and I was terrified. I was keeping ahead of him, in absolute terror, when I came upon a huge ditch and could go no further, I turned around on him - I must have looked crazed, because he turned and ran away. Ann had been racing after the snake, so she came up right behind me. We looked around and realized that we were at a place we did not know, and we were lost. We couldn't get out of the woods. We started yelling for Mama and Daddy, and they had started after us, as we didn't come home right away.

Ann tells the rest better than I do: "And they were calling out, and you were yelling 'Mama' and 'Daddy', and finally they heard your voice. And right in front of us there was this huge circle of just awful briars—and you could get around them very easily, but when you heard Mama's voice, you screamed, 'DON'T LET THAT WOMAN GET AWAY!!!' And you ran right through the briars and scratched yourself all over. I walked around the bush, but you were scratched to pieces."

Another time that I was scared was one afternoon when we had gone over to Wanda Lee's. They had wonderful straw stacks that we used to slide down, and they were as slick as glass.

Ann says, "Over in a field, there was a wonderful pole where we could slide down the straw stack. It was just like glass and I remember there was a bump in the middle. You came down and you hit the bump, and with that, a cow came around the bottom and you landed right on the back of the cow. You slipped off right away, but you were screaming bloody murder."

Because of the terrible times we had had over rabies, Ann and I were never allowed to have a dog again. As a result, we tried to tame other animals there on the farm, and we were successful several times. Our favorite was Cheep-Cheep.

Ann remembers, "Mama used to order chickens, and they would come in a box. We took one of them out and we tamed it, and named it Cheep-Cheep. We could peck on the floor and Cheep-Cheep would come flying. And I remember sitting on the front porch and I had long hair, and he would sit on my shoulder and go to sleep. He was a real pet, and we kept him (or her), apart from all the others. She, I think it turned out to be. At any rate, we took Cheep-Cheep to the springs one day, and we left the window down a little so Cheep-Cheep could get some air. We did something, I don't remember, but I think we got a hotdog or hamburger. We came back to the car and Cheep-Cheep was gone. Cheep-Cheep had gotten out of the window. We went looking everywhere, calling for her all over the place, and finally we heard a weak little 'cheep cheep.' There was this big creek that ran along, which was part of the springs, and it had stones in it. We could step on these to get across. That chicken had gotten in the middle of that stream on one of those rocks and we ran out and got Cheep-Cheep and took her home. And then she got older and older, and finally Mama said that she had to go out with the chickens. In those days Mama killed a chicken every Sunday, and we were scared it would be Cheep-Cheep. For a long time we would go with Mama and we would call 'Cheep-Cheep' and, out of this flock of hens, Cheep-Cheep would come running to us. We could call her and she would still come running."

I remember that popcorn was one of our favorite things, and we didn't get it very often. Every now and then, Mama would pop it for Ann, Jack and me, and we would always have to eat out of the same bowl. We were afraid that one of us would gobble up too much, and we would watch each other like a hawk. So we ate as fast as we possibly could, one grain at a time. Then Daddy would come along and take a big handful, and we would just DIE because we had been sitting there, eating a grain at a time, and he would leave a huge hole in our popcorn.

During this time, Ann, Jack and I would play checkers by taking turns, and then Mama would read to us almost every day. She would put me and Jack on her lap, with Ann sitting on the arm of the chair, and she would take time from her busy day to read. She always had a book going for us.

One thing I remember clearly that happened while we were living up at Fairview. It was during the March electrical storms, and Ann and I were running towards the house because the rain was starting. We looked towards Mom Clift's and could see billows of black smoke, coming from where we thought the house ought to be. We went running in, screaming at Mama that Mom's house was on fire. She ran down to get Charlie Johnson to go with us, and the four of us lit out running in a downpour of rain. As we got closer—she lived just a quarter mile from us—we could tell the smoke was coming from the stable instead of the house, but we didn't let that slow us down. When we got there, Mom Clift was in despair. She had not been able to get all her animals out, as the lightning had hit the stable roof, and had run all the way from the front to the back, with the entire building becoming engulfed in flames almost in seconds. She had gone in once and rescued either a cow or her calf, and some neighbors who had come running over had absolutely stopped her from going back in to get the other one.

Mama was distraught because on the day before, she and Estie had pulled one of Daddy's new pieces of equipment into the barn so it wouldn't get so rusty from setting out. They had done that literally just the day before, and of course, it was burnt to smithereens. Mom said she would not build the stable back there, and she never did.

I can't end this chapter without telling about the only spanking that my Daddy ever gave me. It was when we were living down at Grandmother's, so I was very young.

Ann tells about it better than I ever could: "We were walking home from Grandmother's, and he was mad at you because you hadn't minded him. You had wanted to go up there, and I remember being absolutely terrorized because Daddy had said, 'I wouldn't do that if I were you.' He said that all his life, and it meant "NO". And you went anyway. Your whole defense was, 'I'm not you.' I went up there with him to get you, and coming home he gave you a big swat on your tail."

CHAPTER IX

"FAREWELL TO THE FARM"

In the summer of 1944, Daddy's uncle, Seldon Glenn came to visit. He came in a great big fancy car, and he went into the house to talk to Daddy about a job in Louisville. Just as White was considered the success of Mom Clift's family, Seldon was thought of as the most successful in Grandmother's. His schooling had ended with the third grade, but he had managed to educate himself, and he had become quite influential in the Democratic Party of Kentucky. At one point, he was elected State Senator. Daddy always thought that Uncle Seldon could have kept his job for him at the prison in 1933 had he lifted his hand, and in 1944, Daddy thought he was offering this job with the I.R.S. as an apology for not helping him in the Depression times.

In 1944 Uncle Seldon was the Collector of Internal Revenue for the state of Kentucky, and was able to hand out jobs in the I.R.S. to people that he thought could perform well. His main persuasion towards Daddy was to suggest that Ann and I would be so much better educated in Louisville,

The Way We Were

and we could even live at home throughout college by going to the excellent University of Louisville. This was touching a nerve in Daddy.

When the possibility was put before the family after Uncle Seldon left, Ann and I were horrified, as the thought of leaving Lyon County had never crossed our minds. We raised such a fuss and cried our eyes out, that Daddy wrote to decline the offer. However, a very determined—or very guilty feeling—Uncle Seldon kept after Daddy until he agreed to try it for a while.

Daddy left Lyon County in the fall, and the family followed him in January of 1945. Ann and I had agreed that if we cried day and night to go back, Daddy and Mama would give in, and we would be back in no time. I kept that strategy, but unfortunately for me, Ann became very happy with her quick popularity in the Louisville schools, and I lost half my effectiveness in one fell swoop. It soon became clear to me that we had left the farm forever.

As I stated earlier, one of our favorite books of our childhood was Robert Louis Stevenson's *A Child's Garden of Verses*, and one of the poems we loved best in it was called appropriately "Farewell to the Farm." During the fall of 1944 and all of 1945, I could not begin to read this wonderful poem without crying so hard that I couldn't see the page. I would like to end this book by quoting it here:

Farewell to the Farm

The coach is at the door at last;
The eager children, mounting fast
And kissing hands, in chorus sing:
Good-by, good-by to everything!
To house and garden, field and lawn,
To meadow gates we swung upon,
To pump and stable, tree and swing,
Good-by, good-by to everything!
And fare-you-well for evermore,
Oh ladder at the hayloft door,
Oh hayloft where the cobweb cling,
Good-by, good-by to everything!
Crack goes the whip, and off we go;
The trees and houses smaller grow;
Last, round the woody turn we swing:
Good-by, good-by to everything!

The Way We Were

APPENDIX

The Way We Were

Appendix

MY DAD'S VOCABULARY

Through all my childhood on the farm my Dad loved to use funny comments that suited in his conversation. I never heard him use these comments later in any other case whatsoever. In those early days, they were:

1. "Ahead of the Hounds" - He suggested to us, "If bad news is following you, then try to stay ahead of the hounds." A constant statement.
2. "If I never see the back of my neck again." This he used when his Rook hand was good enough to bid over anybody at the table. Daily.
3. "If God is willing and the Creeks don't rise." Most of the people thought the Creeks were the actual creeks in Lyon County, but my Dad always thought it was about the Creek Indians who were also there. We kids always thought it meant the real creeks of water that we had to try to cross. He was right.
4. "This world and one more, and then comes the fireworks." When bad news comes around, Dad used this all the time when we went to him for help.
5. "God Almighty!!!" He used this whenever he had no better words. He thought that anyone using cusswords were just showing that they had no usable vocabulary - and told them. They showed that they were not smart.

The Way We Were

Appendix

This essay was a final exam at Transylvania University in Lexington in 1993. We were given a tablet and two pencils to write about a place of childhood that we valued the most. We had one hour to finish. I wrote:

A PLACE
Jo Fisher, Oct. 1993

My Grandmother's house burned to the ground almost twenty years ago. No one was living in it at the time, and thus the fire was not as tragic as it might have been. I have been back to Lyon County often during those years, but I have been to the site of where the house had stood only once. What had been the yard was covered with undergrowth and briars with saplings and vines barring the way to trespassers less aggressive than I. It took a while for me to push through to find the remnants of the old concrete front walk, which would show me exactly where the house had been, as it had led directly to the front porch. Underneath the growth, I could discern loose bricks where the chimneys had been. A few feet to the left of what used to be the corner of the house, I could stand on the concrete slab that had been placed over the well of the spring when the house had become abandoned. The memories were overpowering, and I wept at the desolation.

Grandmother's house had been the meeting place of the Jones clan from my earliest recollection, and before that, back

The Way We Were

to the year 1900. The lane leading to it was a narrow dirt road from Fairview School, and when you ran down "rocky hill", you were thrust into "the hollow" which led directly to the "park", as Grandmother liked to call the large front yard.

The house itself was white frame, with five small windows proportionately placed on the second floor, directly over four windows and a front center door at the first level. A central hall led straight through the house to a screened in, long and narrow back porch which was used for sleeping in the dry, hot summers. The porch was the choice spot for hide and seek, and for hiding Easter eggs. We kept a few of Grandfather's watermelons there, and we often chose one early in the morning, carrying it to the cold running creek, securing it in the water, and anxiously waiting for cooler eating.

In the middle of the hall were two doors, one on each side. To the left was "the parlor", the best kept room in this very plain house, where Grandmother had her prized books, her organ, and a place for the less familiar guests to be allowed to sleep. For some reason, on one bitter cold night my sister and I were lifted up into a deep feather mattress that stretched clear across the bed in this room. Quilts were folded over us until we could scarcely turn. Later, I heard a knocking sound after I had been asleep several hours, and when I opened my eyes from the depths of that feather bed, I was looking directly at the ceiling. My Aunt Clara's shadow was there, moving against the light from the coal fire that was burning in the grate. I hunkered down in silence, knowing she would be upset if she knew she had awakened me, and I felt warm and secure in the presence of someone willing to get out of her own bed to come beside mine to stoke up the fire on such a winter's night.

Appendix

On the right side of the hall, the door led into the main room, often called simply "the house". This was the room where a coal fire burned continuously during the winter; where grown-ups sat in their rockers, ringed around the fire, and discussed politics, crops, and family matters. It was in this room the tables were relentlessly put up for Rook in the evenings and the partners were chosen. It was a room filled with love and laughter, faces shining in the glow of the light from the fire and from the kerosine lamps.

This room became even more special at Christmastime, with the smells of cedar and of pine and with the aroma from an over-laden stove permeating the entire house. After supper, Grandmother Jones would gather her nine grandchildren around her chair before the fire, and she would quietly tell us stories. She had a wonderful, rich voice, and she told us her own tales, most of which were not entirely suitable for children, and not always with happy endings. I vaguely remember one about an eagle taking a pearl necklace to its lair, and a child being threatened with dire punishment for its loss until someone happened to spot the necklace. We would all be holding our breaths, wide-eyed, waiting to hear of the vindication, afraid in our hearts that the ending might change at any time and the boy might be punished. This never happened, but we always knew there was the possibility that it might. Grandmother made up her stories as she went along.

The dining room and the kitchen followed this room down the right side of the house, making it a perfect "L" shape. On holidays there would be two full seatings at the huge dining room table, with the children going first. This order was established long ago, so the grown-ups could sit around, drinking coffee, and talking away the long afternoon. Our days seemed carefree, warm and wonderful—and life for me was at its best when I was inside that house.

It seemed strange when I went back a few years ago, to stand where once that house had stood, to walk the perimeter of its walls and to hear the echoing voices of the past, sounding over a now deserted place in a field where only the saplings and the briars grow, disguising entirely the fact that once a house had stood there, holding the lives of the people I loved dearly. The house, the park, the well, the shadows, the stories and the people are all gone now except for that brief afternoon when I stood amongst the bramble and closed my eyes.

ABOUT THE AUTHOR

JONELLE JONES FISHER (Jo) was born in Lyon County, Kentucky, in the summer of 1933. She moved with her family to Louisville when she was twelve years old, and graduated from the University of Louisville in 1954. She and Norman S. (Jack) Fisher married in 1956 just after his sophomore year in medical school. When his training was completed in 1959, they moved with their two children to Midway, Kentucky where he began his practice.

www.ingramcontent.com/pod-product-compliance
Lightning Source LLC
Chambersburg PA
CBHW040230110526
44582CB00001B/2